AFL
Final Day

T0362822

@ the MCG

I am at the game.

My team is the Hawks.

3

My team
jumped for the ball.

5

My team
got the ball.

My team
passed the ball.

My team ran for the ball.
They ran and ran and ran.

My team kicked the ball.

My team dived for the ball.

Go Hawks! Go!

15

I had a great day
at the game.

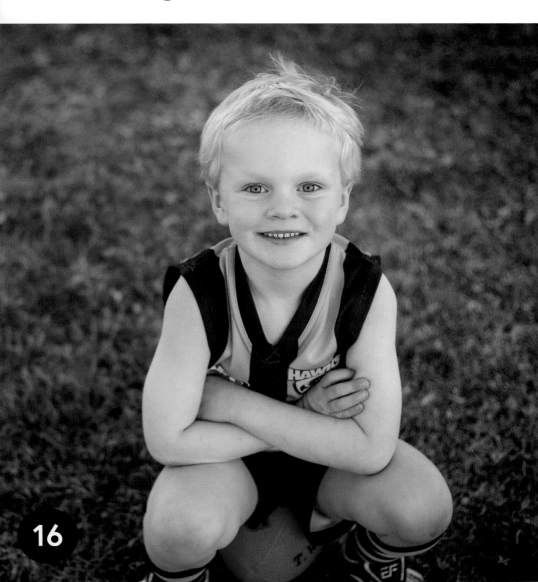